Human Potentials for Change

Dr. Edward Schellhammer

Human Potentials for Change. 1st Edition, 2017.
© Copyright. Dr. Edward Schellhammer.
All rights reserved.

ISBN-13: 978-1975857936
ISBN-10: 1975857933

www.EdwardSchellhammer.com
www.SchellhammerBusinessSchool.com
www.SchellhammerInstitute.com
www.SchellhammerRetreat.com

TABLE OF CONTENTS

FOREWORD

'Modern Philosophical Anthropology' provides the knowledge:

→ For the best possible personal life fulfillment

→ For an evolutionary development of humanity

→ For a new understanding of humans and human development

■ To shape a holistic positive life philosophy

■ To understand oneself and one's inner life

■ To have a realistic and useful concept of man

■ To be able to efficiently use humane knowledge

■ To understand the value of freedom from inside

■ To identify humans' capacities and potentials

■ To understand the human interrelations

■ To identify the genuine spiritual values

■ To find the concept of true meaning of life

■ To identify the factors of sustainable collective peace

- To form a concept for efficiently exploring inner worlds
- To understand the roots of the innermost human values
- To find an advanced, realistic, useful spiritual concept
- To find the sustainable (self-) education for a successful life
- To constructively deal with the manifoldness of humans
- To identify the real criteria for the truth about humans

The Tasks of Philosophical Anthropology

A modern Philosophical Anthropology aspires for a holistic approach and a multidimensional understanding of humans' development, human's life and humanity's evolution.

A modern Philosophical Anthropology serves to

prepare the humans for efficient, constructive and evolutionary ways of life, of mastering life and making a fulfilling living.

A modern Philosophical Anthropology serves for politics and economics, for public education and religions to find completely new concepts and ways of solution of the dire global problems.

Such a position includes relevant normative orientations about essential humane dimensions:

- To live with a holistic positive life philosophy with real hope.
- To understand our feelings and to be able to manage them.
- To live love, our genuine psychical needs, with truthfulness.
- To see through, to think profoundly and also in creative ways.

- To understand ourselves, our inner life, and our behavior.

- To acquire knowledge and skills to efficiently master life.

- To become an authentic, fully self-realized and strong person.

- To have real, efficient, constructive ideals, values, norms, and rules.

- To live a new, authentic life style with an excellent self-management.

- To prepare ourselves for a happy relationship and family life.

- To live our desire for the other gender, for sex, for love and trust.

- To live free from biographical burdens and unconscious complexes.

- To be able to solve difficulties, crises, problems, and conflicts.

- To praise and to live the deepest eternal meaning of marriage.

- To succeed with our children by making them authentic and strong.

- To live and grow with a genuine meaning of life that is rooted inside.

- To understand our dreams, messages from the spiritual intelligence.

- To correctly meditate and practice mental training for wellness.

- To live the fundamental inner processes for the complete fulfillment.

- To care for health, humans, environment, humanity and the planet.

- Obviously these statements are already the result of a modern Philosophical Anthropology.

- These dimensions are the indispensable important topics of Philosophical Anthropology.

- It doesn't make sense to create a Philosophical Anthropology without these dimensions.

- Such a new modern Philosophical Anthropology can provide a sustainable education.

- A Philosophical Anthropology that does not consider psychical-spiritual evolution is scrap.

1. HUMANS IN HISTORIC VIEW

Human images developed in the history are:

- A human is 'de nature' good and bad.
- A human is the Lupus of humans.
- A human is the double (copy) of God.
- A human is a being that can will.
- A human is the sick animal.
- A human is an uncompleted creature.
- A human is a social being.
- A human is the animal that can beat.
- A human is a biological being.
- A human is the result of external influences.
- A human is the being that can think.
- A human is the highest creation of God.
- A human is lazy, incalculable, a liar, egoistic.
- A human is a spiritual being.

- A human is a being that can create culture.

- A human is talented to create techniques.

- A human is a being with reason.

- A human is a gambler.

- A human is able to love.

- A human is disposed to be formed and educated.

- A human is the being that can sin.

- A human is a pure race or impure race.

- A human is a learning organism.

A human is not simply a human by biological shape. There are several multidimensional ways to describe humans. All humans have the same biological and mental structures. There are billions of humans shaped in billions of ways.

- We can't determine the 'human' without the mind (the 'psyche').

- A human also must be understood under behavioral dimensions.

- Social interactions form part of the understanding of humans.
- Meaning and spiritual values essentially determine humans.
- The human also must be understood with environmental factors.
- Determining the 'human' leads to the meaning of human's life.

2. ETHICS AND HUMAN EVOLUTION

From the ethical perspective modern Philosophical Anthropology also deals with:

- Analysis of superficiality, lies, life lies, cheat, falseness, bigotry, rigidity, narcissism, big mouths, stubbornness, arrogance, ignorance, unreasonableness, sadism, disrespect, stone-cold coolness and scrupulousness.
- Analysis of people that poison humanity with their immorality, blown up ego, megalomania,

perversion, dogmatism and fundamentalism, superstition, lunacy, madness, psychopathy, extreme greed, evil purposes, and religious psychosis.

- Analysis of being deceived, lured, brainwashed and manipulated, oppressed and led into sick meanders, exploited as a human and financially abused like slaves, treated as vacuous soulless humans to make a few selected individuals into super-billionaires.

- Analysis of pollution, contamination, climate change, environmental destruction, exploitation of resources, speculations, global poverty and misery, injustice, nuclear waste, political practices, armament, wars, fascism and the new Nazi-like laws and practices.

- Analysis of façades or masks that hide or distort realities; 'de natura' humans don't want to be the puppets of politicians and the economy, the corporations or religions and humans don't want to be detracted from the truth and misled with false promises.

→ Most words in the above statements have a negative value and connotation.

→ A healthy mind will never want that such critical moral qualities dominate life.

→ A fundamental, practical ethics is indispensable for the evolution of humanity.

■ Modern Philosophical Anthropology operates with an intrinsic ethics which is rooted in the holistic understanding of humans' evolution.

■ As a normative statement the ethic principals consider such critical aspects as condemnable as they operate in destructive ways against human development.

3. THE MIND AND ITS FUNCTIONS

Philosophical Anthropology is to do with humans and

humans' life. Philosophical Anthropology can't properly describe a human without mental dimensions and the interrelation with human's behavior and the environment. A human is also specified through meaning. Everything that has a non-material meaning is 'spiritual'. What is a human without a psychical life? He is a mere human biomass. What is a human without a spiritual life? He is a mere human biomass.

Human evolution leads to decay if the mental and spiritual potentials are ignored.

Some facts about psychical life are:

- A lot in life has psychical origins and effects.
- Each human being has a psychical life.
- Each person has a lot of singular psychical forces.
- Human behavior is linked with psychical forces.
- A human being is a psychical-spiritual being.
- Human life is predominantly meaning-oriented.

- A person never finds his authentic self-fulfillment without forming his psychical-spiritual life.
- Without self-education there are unbalanced results with extensive critical consequences.
- No knowledge, pre-judgments, and indifference paralyzes a person, makes him blind.

The main mental (psychical-spiritual) systems:

➔ The 'I' (ego, self) with its supportive functions
➔ The defense, integration, will, control
➔ The cognition (thinking)
➔ The emotions (feelings)
➔ The genuine inner needs
➔ The unconscious mind
➔ The love capacity
➔ The spiritual intelligence (dreams)

- Every result of behavior and mental activity in humans' life depends on the kinds of the formed psychical-spiritual functions.

- As humans are intrinsically spiritual, they destroy humans' evolution if they ignore the spiritual meaning and values.

- Also business, politics, economics, spirituality and religion have indispensably and primordially to do with the mental functions.

- All religions (but also atheism) are fundamentally the result of the ways how humans' psychical-spiritual functions are shaped.

- What happens with humans that are not well formed in all their mental functions?

<u>Model of Human's Mind:</u>

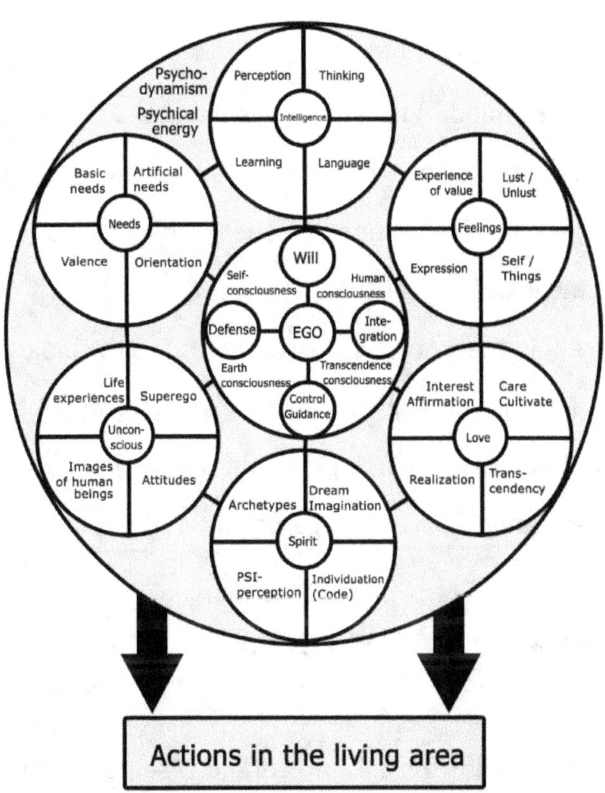

- The mind is a vivid psychical-spiritual organism and never a measurable and calculable human machine. The complexity of this organism makes a human 'humane'.

- All systems of the mind are in interaction; they influence each other in a constructive or critical way. The lack of formed mental quality has immense consequences.

- The mind identifies and creates 'meaning'. Therefore the mind is never simply a sum of psychical functions. In that sense humans are intrinsically 'spiritual'.

- All humans are intrinsically not only biological and psychological, but also 'spiritual'. The biological, psychological and spiritual dimensions are an inseparable organic unity.

4. HUMAN VALUES TODAY

Modern Philosophical Anthropology searches for and analyzes genuine human values and mental qualities.

➜ A human life and a society without genuine human values is an insane perversion.

→ A human life with low and very low mental qualities has always critical effects.

→ There is no sustainable success in human's life without formed human values.

→ Constructive ways of living and mental operations promote humans' evolution.

→ It is not possible that all human values are at any time satisfied, actual or vivid.

■ Absence of genuine human values leads to the destruction of humanity's evolution.

■ Low mental qualities are inefficient, hinder and destroy human's life and evolution.

■ A human life with much reduced human values is misery, darkness, and mere pain.

The state of humanity and the planet shows us:

- There is an immense absence of human values.
- There is an immense lack of spiritual education.
- There is an immense lack of mental qualities.

- There is an immense lack of knowledge about the mind.

- There is an immense lack of efficient mental functions.

- There is an immense distortion of humans' core meaning of life.

- There is an immense disrespect for humans' evolution.

5. DIMENSIONS OF HUMAN CONCEPTS

There are many dimensions that can be explored to understand the species 'human'.

There are innumerable institutions and millions of people that explore these dimensions.

Everywhere they claim to have the right knowledge and concepts.

A majority of them are 'accredited' and 'recognized'

from highest authorities.

But all their knowledge and skills have not been able to create an evolutionary humanity.

Something must be fundamentally wrong with these institutions and people.

→ Modern humans explore the earth, the biology, the material, nano-worlds, and the universe, but have a very primitive understanding about humans and in particular about themselves.

→ Modern sciences explore the mind and behavior of humans in order to enslave, brainwash, manipulate and exploit humans, but never to find the genuine meaning of humans' life.

→ Modern concepts of spirituality, sects and all religions essentially ignore or abuse the advanced knowledge about humans; in particular they don't promote holistic evolution.

- The genuine aims of Social Sciences are to understand the species 'human' and humanity as a whole in all its dimensions, including the intrinsic genuine meaning of life.
- Social Sciences should promote human's evolution, human values, human potentials, qualities of mind and behavior and society's culture aiming an all-sided balanced individual and collective evolution. But they do not.

Human behavior is related to the human's mind.

- → The mind is the operational center of human's behavior.
- → The quality of behavior depends on the quality of the mind's operation.
- → The content of the unconscious mind has an immense influence in behavior.
- → Psychotic and dogmatic belief directs behavior into anti-evolutional processes.

- The kind of forming of the mental functions determines human's behavior.

- An imbalanced or malformed mind always leads to critical behavior.

- Lack of awareness of meaning and spiritual values leads to destructive behavior.

- Forming and re-forming the mental functions is a lifelong requirement.

6. SELF-KNOWLEDGE

Self-knowledge is the key topic of modern Philosophical Anthropology:

- Most people know themselves on a level of 3-5 %; the rest they avoid to see.

- Most people don't think about their tomorrow or the inner network of their way of living.

- Most people believe that they are totally right with the way they think and judge.

- Most people have no idea about their unconscious inner world – their true being.
- Most people believe it is enough what they have learnt; but it's only blind obstinacy.
- Most people can't distinguish between infatuated appearance and realities.
- Most people want to be cheated spiritually, religiously, ideologically, or esoterically.
- Most people don't want to learn for love, spirit, joy, happiness, peace and balance.
- Most people don't have the necessary knowledge and skills for their self-fulfillment.

→ But the importance of self-knowledge is of indisputable value and utility. Self-knowledge:

- Forms key qualification for personal and professional life
- Establishes competences for relationship and life in general

- Reduces many life risks and suffering in the lifetime
- Is applicable everywhere, gives foundation, dynamically stabilizes the self-identity
- Includes elaborated knowledge about humans and life, acting and environment
- Qualifies for the right use of leisure, lifetime and personal potentials
- Creates inner security and trust in one's own forces and self-identity
- Forms an all-sided balanced psychical organism in permanent progression
- Is indispensable to find enrichment and substantial fulfillment
- Integrates high ethical responsibility for oneself, others, work, society, the planet
- Is an investment for the future, also in the context of the big problems of humanity
- Is indispensable in the fields of education, management, care, guiding people

- Reaches the innermost being of humans, also in the decisive spiritual questions
- Is indispensable in the future for all kinds of professional activities

→ A human with low and very low self-knowledge is an archaic human.

→ A human with low and very low self-knowledge is a destructive human.

→ A human without self-knowledge can never live in an evolutionary process.

→ A scientist or expert of Philosophical Anthropology needs self-knowledge.

- Without self-knowledge a human can never find the 'truth' about human's life.
- A human with low and very low self-knowledge never reaches his fulfillment.
- Without self-knowledge a human can never grow psychologically and spiritually.

- A scientist of Philosophical Anthropology without self-knowledge talks rubbish.
- Mental functions and self-knowledge create religion, not the other way round.

Importance of Self-Knowledge:

→ Lack of self-knowledge or weak and low self-knowledge always has critical consequences.

→ 7 billion people with low or lack of self-knowledge lead humanity towards the abyss.

→ The development of a human without management of self-knowledge creates disasters.

→ There is never genuine happiness and personal fulfillment without profound self-knowledge.

→ A relationship between man and woman without rigorous self-knowledge ends in sadness.

→ Lack of self-knowledge is the most essential part of stupidity, arrogance, mental disorder.

- Self-knowledge is the supreme call for all humans to be and to become a genuine human.
- A religion and any concept of spirituality without a thorough self-knowledge are a scam.

7. DESTRUCTIVITY OF SPECIES AND HUMANS

- An animal doesn't unlimitedly kill other animals.
- An eagle doesn't kill (and eat) an elephant.
- A dog doesn't kill a lion.
- Animals kill and eat until they are satisfied.
- Plants do not destroy the planet and the eco-systems.
- Plants don't kill other plants.
- Animals do not destroy the planet and its eco-systems.
- Animals don't destroy the place of other animals for perverse pleasure.
- Animals don't destroy or kill because of hate, greed, malicious joy, lust, insanity, etc.

→ The world of species expresses multiple balance.

→ Animals and plants don't eat unlimitedly.

→ Animals and plants don't kill deliberately for lust.

→ Animals and plants don't destroy the planet.

Humans compared with animals:

- Humans (can) eat countless plants and animals, nearly everything that is not toxic.

- More than one billion humans eat much more than they need to be satisfied.

- More than a billion humans eat much more than their stomach's capacity.

- Humans destroy the eco-systems, the resources, and with that the planet.

- Humans kill unlimitedly other humans, babies, children, adults, women, men, etc.

- Humans destroy unlimited alien infrastructure simply to destroy their livelihood.

- Humans destroy and kill because of hate, greed, malicious joy, lust, insanity, etc.

- The world of humans has a tendency to ignore or destroy any multiple balances.

- Humans eat unlimitedly and far beyond the need of biological satisfaction.
- Humans eat even if they are not hungry, simply to get a compensatory satisfaction.
- Humans deliberately destroy livelihood and kill other humans, often without limit.
- Humans destroy unstoppably and irreversibly the eco-systems and the planet.
- Some humans aim to control the entire humanity and to dominate the evolution.

➜ Is this the nature of humans or the result of a malformed mind?

➜ A malformed mind is in the long term always unlimitedly destructive.

Becoming a human:

- A human starts to exist on earth with the unification of an ovule cell and sperm.

- Becoming a human begins with the biological process of development and growth.

- The entire coding to become a human is embedded in the ovule cell and sperm cell.

- The concept of a human lies in the DNA codes that contain all information to grow.

- It's a masterwork that such an outstanding concept creates our existence on earth.

Procreating a baby affects society, the world, the eco-systems, the planet and humanity. Humans start to exist through an ovule and sperm. Humans forget that their existence is limited. With the increase of the world population also the global problems increase. A majority of humans are not well formed in the mind, so they destroy the planet.

➜ It's a unique gift to be a human, to be on earth, to make a living, and to grow lifelong.

→ Humans go through very different and unique life periods starting as an embryo.

→ The kinds of development are innumerable: biological, psychical, spiritual, and behavioral.

→ The manifoldness of experiences humans can make during their life on earth is amazing.

→ Positive and negative life experiences shape and determine humans' development.

→ The human's existence on earth is not due to a merit; it's a result of the nature's capacity.

- All humans start and live their life under the conditions of the planet.

- All humans start and live their life under the condition of DNA codes.

- All humans start and live their life under specific environmental conditions.

- All humans start and live their life influenced by experiences since prenatal time.

- All humans start, develop and live under the condition of their formed mind.

- All humans grow and live under the condition of the organs' inner clocks.

8. HUMANS' BIOLOGY

- A human is biologically determined by his physical body.
- Specific cells form together a specific organ, each with specific functions.
- Together, all cells and organs enable the body (and mind) to function.
- All organs and cells have some kind of inner clock regulating their functions.
- The entire body of a human has a kind of biorhythm humans can respect or ignore.
- Humans must eat, drink and take care of their body in order to be healthy.
- There are chemical elements in the environment that can produce malfunctions.
- There are toxic elements in the environment that can seriously damage or kill.

- An increased cocktail of alien chemical elements in the body will kill humans.

- All humans need some kind of housing, physically and psychologically indispensable.

In the modern worlds of today:

→ Many Humans ignore bodily needs and limits.

→ Most people ignore the rhythm of the inner clock.

→ A majority of humans ignore their biorhythm.

→ Most people don't care about their body's health.

→ Billions suffer from hunger and dirty water.

→ Up to 400 alien chemical elements in the body.

→ Humans create their toxic environment.

→ More than a billion people don't have a shelter.

- All humans need healthy food and healthy water, housing and healthy environment.

- Absence of healthy food and water, housing and a healthy environment dehumanizes.

- There is no food, partly no water, and no appropriate housing without humans' work.
- A healthy environment today requires human's responsibility and corresponding work.

9. THE GENDER DIFFERENCES

Prejudgments:

a) Man: rigid, violent, quarrelsome, pugnacious, authoritarian, imperious, domineering, etc.

b) Women: inconsiderate, moody, irrational, sensible, hysterical, seductive, etc.

- Male characteristics are: spirit, structure, projects, management, orgasmic sex, principles, exploration, beget life, analytical thinking, rational power.
- Female characteristics are: Life, Care for, Nourish, protect, look after, sensitivity, receive, romantic

sex, intuitive thinking, to give life, emotional power.

Thesis for the man:

If a man cannot form his masculine principles in a balance and orientation with feminine principles, so he is a destructive man and not a developed man.

Thesis for the woman:

If a woman cannot form her feminine principles in a balance and orientation with masculine principles, so she is a destructive woman and not a developed woman.

10. DIFFERENT EDUCATION

We can identify the educational status by different levels:

- Illiterates and semi-illiterates
- Educational preparation: kindergarten

- Low education: only primary school (4 or 6 years)

- Standard graduation: secondary school

- Vocational education

- High School: Preparation for academic study

- University: Enables for specific worlds

We can identify the educational status from premise perspective:

- Poor or primitive educational premises and methods or tools

- Luxurious educational premises and methods or tools

→ Whatever the educational status of humans is, they are all humans.

→ Poor or luxurious educational premises, both are for humans' education.

→ Pre-school education aims to promote mental and social capacities.

→ Basic and secondary (non-)public education is for enabling to make a living.

→ Vocational school is indispensable in order to work with knowledge and skills.

→ Academic education is a preparation for professions with high knowledge and skills.

- Education always shapes humans in their personality and ways of living.
- Education is indispensable for growing and making a living and mastering life.
- Humans develop and become a human through a variety of education.
- Quality of educational premises can have effects in positive or negative direction.
- Humans need vocational education for working attitudes, knowledge, and skills.
- Public education fully ignores the psychical-spiritual development of humans.
- A huge majority of politicians ignore the importance of psychical-spiritual development.

- Economics fully ignore the values and necessity of psychical-spiritual development.
- Religions fully ignore the archetypal psychical-spiritual development of humans.
- Educational status says nothing about the status of psychical-spiritual development.

11. DIFFERENT PROFESSIONS

There is a manifold variety of professional education.

→ Whatever the professional education and work is focused on, they are all humans.

→ The manifoldness of professional education and work shapes human's life.

→ Working always includes knowledge, skills, working attitudes, responsibility, and so on.

→ Malformed mental and spiritual functions drastically reduce the working capacity.

→ Reduced health and miserable working conditions leads into fatal humane criticalities.

- Working (performance) is a genuine need, indispensable for life and human's evolution.

- Work is not simply a job to get money, but also part of psychical-spiritual development.

- Longer unemployment, underemployment or absence of work options dehumanizes.

- Not providing work to all humans results in the destruction of humans' mind and life.

- Immense absence of work options puts society and human's evolution at serious risk.

- Huge absence of work shows the incompetence and madness of politics and economics.

- Professional status says nothing about the status of psychical-spiritual development.

- The manifold variety of professions allows to live manifold potentials and talents.

- All professions always shape the working person mentally and spiritually in some ways.

12. LEADERSHIP AND AUTHORITY

Any community, group, cooperation, institution in society is build up as a pyramid. On the top are the leaders and authorities. Nothing is wrong with that.

- A human can be charged of any collective responsibility.
- A human can be a top manager (CEO).
- A human can be an authority in religions.
- A human can be an authority in politics.
- A human can be an authority in economics.
- A human can be an authority in health care.
- A human can be an authority in jurisdiction.
- A human can be a military general.
- A human can be a supreme authority.
- A human can be an aristocrat or a king (queen).
- A human can be a president, prime minister...

➜ Whatever the authority status is, these humans remain to be a human.

➔ The kind of authority status decisively shapes the office holders.

➔ The work of an authority can't be better than his mental state is.

➔ A mad authority produces insanity in his society, often worldwide.

➔ Mentally imbalanced leaders and authorities always create misery.

➔ Professional expertise is never enough for a sustainable leadership.

■ Abuse of leadership and of legitimate authority leads to collective disasters.

■ Lack of integrity (moral character), relevant knowledge and skills leads to disasters.

■ Highly neurotic, psychopathic, psychotic, insane leaders (authorities) destroy humanity.

■ Absence or low level of personal psychical-spiritual growth leads to catastrophes.

13. ARCHAIC HUMAN BEING

The essential characteristics of an 'archaic human being' are:

- Ignoring the psyche as the genuine life; therefore no holistic development
- Rejecting the inner Spirit and the performance potential of the power of love
- Pushed from suppressed burdens and in the tendency projecting strongly
- Not living with dreams, imagination, contemplation, and introspection
- Only partially conscious forming of the psychical forces – if at all
- Defense from and suppression of all uncomfortable, weak and different realities
- To a large extent an unconscious way of living without being aware of the psychical life
- Personal and life culture are rooted in ideologies, dogmas and fundamentalism

- Extensively being fixed on material goods, events (fun), and external securities
- Undifferentiated unilateral experiencing of love, lust and sensuality
- Performances with increase of gain and the extreme have highest value

Negative forming: archaic

Not much learning; undifferentiated; unconscious; disordered, not organized; badly controlled; unbalanced; incalculable; destructive; one-sided; suppressed; defensive.

- Humans must become aware of the archaic characteristics.
- Humans have the freedom to decide about archaic forming.

14. EVOLUTIONARY HUMAN BEING

The essential characteristics of an 'evolutionary human being' are:

- Accepting the psychical life and a conscious forming of all psychical forces

- Liberation from inner burdens of the biography and becoming free from projecting dynamics

- Elaborated images in the unconscious constructively and progressively promoting life

- Continuous inner orientation through dream interpretation, imagination and contemplation

- Integration and elaboration of all the uncomfortable, weak and different 'things' in life

- Creating relationships, politics and economy (etc.) from the understanding of Individuation

- Dealing with nature and the world of animals, and the environment with Spirit and love

- Differentiated development and use of the power of love and the Spirit

- High flexibility and inner freedom towards material goods and external values
- Psychical-spiritual performances, characterized by love and Spirit have highest values

Positive forming: evolutionary development

Learning; differentiated; conscious; ordered; organized; balanced; controlled; calculable; constructive; manifold; considered; Integrative.

- Humans must become aware of the evolutionary characteristics.
- Humans have the freedom to decide about evolutionary forming.

Direction of Evolution:

- Integration of psychical life
- Tied to holistic inner development
- Being conscious about inner life

- Order in the psychical life

- Constructive psychical forces

- Expansion in quality

- Living tied to the inner Spirit

- Power to balanced guidance

- Life dedicated (love for life)

- Progressive development

- Open to learn, to renewal

- Flexible at disposal

- Clarified and structured

- Clear and differentiated

- Many-sided balanced

- Controllable from 'I'

- Integrated into consciousness

- Dynamic balancing

- Consciously reflected/analyzed

- Integrating, promoting life

- Calculable

- Negative dispositions and developments destroy humanity's evolution (development).

- ■ Up to 90% of all humans are on a negative track towards destruction.

15. THE PROCESS OF INDIVIDUATION

Growing continuously and evolutionarily means:

1. Progression in the human being includes: Objectivity, acceptance, integration, system, order, liberty, spirit, love, life acceptance, dedication, care, balance, responsibility.

2. In the collective unconscious there is something like an 'oath' which 'obliges' all human beings to believe: "The evolutionary, psychical-spiritual human being doesn't exist."

3. If you want to live an authentic self-realization, then you have to know yourself well and the consequences must lead to concrete actions.

4. The alternative to Individuation is: regression, unconscious being, to ignore, without spirit,

negation of life, reduction of life, self-alienation, archaism, dogmatism, and fundamentalism.

5. Experiences of the individuation process are: openness, honesty, seriousness, objectivity, authenticity, reconciliation, relief, humanity, self-responsibility.

6. Everyone can find hundreds of reasons against Individuation; and at least one reason for Individuation: the well-balanced development of the psychical-spiritual human being.

→ A person can deny his psychical-spiritual world.

→ Mankind can negate the force of love.

→ Humans can live without spiritual intelligence.

→ A person can suppress all mental functions.

→ People can destroy and hate all humanity.

→ All humans can bind on external facts / objects such as goods, power, ideologies, dogmas, laws, leaders as a compensation for self-fulfillment.

- Mankind is still at the beginning of the collective evolutional process.

- Most people rarely know what of all the vivid psychical realities can actually be formed.

- Mankind still widely lives at the level of the archaic human being.

- Where shall humans find answers to their basic questions of the existence if not in their psychical organism and through experiencing the inner psychical-spiritual evolution?

The Archetypal Processes of the Soul:

First phase:

1. The complete acceptance of the inner life and the dedication towards it.

2. The discovery and formation of psychical forces and functions.

3. The formation and living of the genuine inner self through conscious formation.

<u>Second phase:</u>

4. The integration of the inner Spirit as a guiding power (dreams, meditation).

5. Carrying out the process of "dying and rebirth" (renewal).

6. The development of the unification with the inner opposite gender pole.

<u>Third phase:</u>

7. Integrating the spiritual principles in ethics, behavior and meaning of life.

8. Bringing the inner and outer world into a balance, anchored within.

9. Achieving the fulfillment of wholeness and completeness (Aim).

➜ Individuation is complete with these Archetypal Processes of the Soul.

The Archetypal experiences express themselves in dreams and are the result of spiritual, psychical, theoretical, meditative and practical processes, including a lot of experience and learning about life, human beings, societies, cultures, humanity and the state of the earth.

- Archetypes are instruments that help in finding orientation in the Individuation.
- Archetypes stimulate forces, growth and development.
- Archetypes order psychical forces in new structures and new interconnections.
- Archetypes open and light up new inner realities.
- Archetypes represent the eternally valid psychical-spiritual process and realities.
- Archetypes facilitate intercultural communication about these realities.
- Archetypes also lead to experiences about the 'mystery' of man and God.
- Archetypes are the very old images of a transcendental reality.

- Archetypes of the soul are also energetic 'transformers'.

- The Archetypes of the Soul are the highest orientation for humanity, for religion, spirituality, politics, economy, industry and education.

- The Archetypes of Individuation are special genuine images of the soul, well known since the beginning of the first cultures.

- The archetypal images are culturally independent image-patterns, most probably first procreated from dreams, from the spiritual source of the soul (the unconscious being).

- The Archetypes of the Soul contain an eternally valid meaning about human being, human life, meaning of life interconnected with the nature of the psyche (soul) and the characteristics of human life from procreation till death.

- Archetypes of the Soul can never been extinguished. In that sense they are 'holy', 'untouchable', and valid for all humans today and in the future.

- ■ There are higher Archetypes of the Soul which are related to professional, spiritual (or religious) 'missions'.

16. ARCHETYPES IN DREAMS

Archetypes are expressed in symbolic sceneries and actions (dreams):

- Circle-cross-Mandala, pentagram, pyramid, square, triangle
- Chalice, vessel, philosopher's stone, Holy Grail, chalice of the Grail, sword of the King of the Grail
- King, queen; celebration of coronation, of getting a 'bond' and corresponding insignia
- Birth, the new human being, a new land
- Sun, moon, light, source (well)
- Owl, speaking snake, eagle, lion, tiger, elephant
- Tree (life tree), garden (paradise)

- Cottage, chateau, castle, temple, 'holy' places

- Going on a voyage (long peregrination), going to 'school' (Accepting the psychical spiritual inner world and path)

- Discovering the psyche: searching for the treasure, investigation of a cave, shadow like persons, or going in deep darkness (a wood, a mysterious place).

- New birth: Birth of a child, a baby is suddenly there, Christmas, opening something new.

- Accepting the inner Spirit: Initiation, consecration, receiving insignia or new clothing.

- Transformation: To die, funeral, farewell, coming to a new land.

- Unification: marriage, embracement with a fairy, entering into a sun, experiencing a special light.

- New spiritual norms / principles: Insignia of a king, a wise person, a new land, new laws.

- Harmony interior-exterior, transcendence, melody, hexagram, light, warmth.

- Wholeness: Circle, Mandala, sun, eternal fire as an ancient source of life, being in a paradise.

Humans can easily abuse the archetypal meaning (symbols):

➜ In leadership

➜ In jurisdiction

➜ In politics

➜ In economics

➜ In social life

➜ In ceremonies

➜ In religion

➜ In spiritual concepts

➜ In esoteric

➜ In social sciences

- The abuse or absence of the Archetypes of the Soul leads to the elimination of humanity's evolution.

- Politics, economics, public education, and religions around the globe entirely practice the abuse of the Archetypes of the Soul.

- Most people admire those who abuse the Archetypes of the Soul; or they are unable to see the value of the genuine and vivid Archetypes of the Soul.

17. NEW LIFE PERSPECTIVES

Constructive perspective:

- Forming all psychical functions is a natural need of every human being.
- The forming of a function must be in an adequate relation to the other functions.
- The most valuable aim of life is an all-sided balanced state of all functions.
- Suppressing and neglecting singular functions always has a destructive effect.

- The inner Spirit is informative, corrective, educative, supportive, and normative.
- The most essential meaning of life is forming the psychical-spiritual organism.
- Love is as essential as intelligence for living and realizing the meaning of life.
- Ideals, values, and norms must be in an appropriate network with these functions.

Critical perspective:

- Everything excessive and over-dominant by ignoring other functions is destructive.
- The unconscious world is more powerful than the conscious mind and ego.
- An unelaborated unconscious means disequilibrium and is always destructive.
- An unelaborated collective unconscious produces wars and world destruction.
- A claim to power by ignoring the aim of an all-sided balanced being is destructive.

- The qualities and values of all the functions must be higher than external values.

→ There is never a new life without a new understanding of human's mind.

→ There is never a new life without a new holistic public education.

→ There is never a new life without new holistic governance (politics).

→ There is never a new life without a new holistic religion (spirituality).

→ There is never a new life without new authentic ways of living.

Consequences:

- Real life today demands extensive formation processes of all psychical functions.
- Ignoring authentic and genuine growth and living ends in illness and destructivity.
- There is no peace, no happiness, and no fulfillment without this educational process.

- The state of humanity and the earth is an expression of the results of wrong education.

- Giving priority to fun, assets, reputation, prestige, and power destroys humanity.

- The state of humanity and the earth is an expression of the results of fake religions.

<u>Aims and Meaning of Life:</u>

The aims:

- to understand the way of operating your conscious and unconscious being has

- to elaborate the heavy and hindering aspects of your biography

- to become new from the bottom of your being and to integrate your potentials

- to transform the opposites, ambivalences, unbalances and shadows

- to become free from all unconscious complexes and suppressed conflicts

- to form the inner balance of the polarity to the other gender
- to grow to an all-sided balanced unity and totality
- to live with love, Spirit, mind, intelligence, wisdom and skills
- to achieve your far-reaching self-fulfillment as your inner destiny
- to discover your destiny; and to realize your prominent visions
- to elaborate and fulfill all archetypal processes of the Individuation
- to go through all the processes of superior spiritual (religious) vocations

→ Personal development is an indispensable condition for any kind of success in life.

→ A life without personality education is archaic, unconscious, chaotic, and full of failure.

→ A natural and undisturbed, not influenced development of a person doesn't exist.

→ Many mental functions forming a person stay out of the person's control.

→ Without knowledge and elaboration of the experiences and without a holistic self-education, no self-determination can be realized.

→ Ignoring genuine aims makes a person dependent on ideologies, dogmas, pre-judgments, and institutions, other people, and one's own unconscious.

<u>Ideals of Humans:</u>

(Based on the psychical organism)

Most people have an ideal of the positive personality. Modern Philosophical Anthropology reflects ideals related to the mind, to behavior, to ways of living, and to the environment:

1. All-included extensive self-knowledge
2. Differentiated self-image

3. Clear many-sided knowledge about humans and the world

4. Understanding of transcendence through psychical-spiritual growth

5. Experiencing existence in the complexity of all inner and external worlds

6. Strong, dynamic and positive Self-experience

7. Free of defense mechanism and projection, but a flexible borderline

8. Open, dynamic integration of all realities of life

9. Strong, consciously formed will

10. Formed self-control in the complexity of inner and external worlds

11. Completely elaborated unconscious life

12. Differentiated perception of one's own and of others realities

13. Creative, constructive thinking with clear language (words)

14. Open to learn and steadily ready to change and extend

15. Clear and balanced satisfied inner needs

16. Many-sided balanced emotional life

17. Sustainable and operational ability to love in all life areas

18. Flexible and vital psychodynamic, free of cramped opposites

19. Intensive communication with the inner Spirit (dreams, meditation)

20. Daily acting in reflection with the entire psychical organism

21. Development of the psychical-spiritual organism with love and Spirit

22. To live and to become a vivid copy of the archetype of fulfillment

- Behavior is always related to the mind. Therefore, it doesn't make sense to develop a modern Philosophical Anthropology without relating to and understanding the mind.

- Religions without such ideals of personality (of humans) act beyond the mind and therefore are inefficient and collectively self-destructive.

Human Education:

Modern Philosophical Anthropology is the foundation of human education:

- Exploring, understanding and forming all psychical forces and its interplay.
- Catharsis, order, renewal, correction of all psychical forces; restructuration.
- Holistic growth of all psychical forces in the orientation of the archetypes of the soul.
- Abilities to master crises, conflicts, disturbances, difficulties and suffering.
- Living is always rooted in the authentic inner life and balanced with the external life.

Wrong, inadequate or lack of human education leads to immeasurable criticalities.

➜ Public education does not consider all these critical consequences.

➜ Religion does not consider all these critical consequences.

➜ Public education and religion do not form humans for mastering life.

➜ Public education and religion do not form humans for a holistic development.

➜ The modern economics does not consider all these critical consequences.

➜ Academic education is completely separated from human education.

■ Most humans are not aware of such immense consequences of wrong education.

■ Most humans are not aware of the importance of life long education and self-forming.

■ Humans are not aware that they are fundamentally shaped already in the prenatal time.

Pillars of Human Education:

Plan and Principles:

➜ The complete acceptance of the inner life and the dedication towards it.

➜ The discovery and formation of psychical forces and functions.

➜ The formation and living of the genuine inner self through formation.

➜ The integration of the inner Spirit as a guiding power (dreams, meditation).

➜ Carrying out the process of 'dying and rebirth' (all-encompassing renewal).

➜ The development of the unification with the inner opposite gender pole.

➜ Integrating the spiritual principles in ethics, behavior and meaning of life.

➜ Bringing the inner and outer world into a balance, anchored within.

➜ Achieving the fulfillment of wholeness and completeness (Individuation).

The characteristic of a mature personality:

- Extended perception of psychical and real world

- Acceptance of oneself, of others and of nature

- Cooperation, promotion, growth

- Spontaneity and authenticity in relationships

- A good and clear focus on problems

- Flexible way of dealing with conflicts

- Flexible distance and yearning for privacy

- Autonomy and resistance against influences

- Deep understanding of emotional expressions

- High frequency of experiencing human values

- Psychical and spiritual openness for people

- Democratic and partnership-like character

- Strong and manifold creativity to express love

- Fairness, objectivity, truthfulness, trust, reliability

- Humility, realistic self-image, wisdom

- Attitudes of permanent learning (never ending)

- Beauty (of the character), style, orderliness

- Balance between rational- spiritual intelligence

- Inner substantial deepness (profoundness)

- Respect for humanity, nature, world of animals

- Always searching for the truth, for balance
- Centered, rooted in the inner Spirit

Fundamental pillars of personality education are:

- Forming and understanding all psychical forces and its interplay.
- Order, correction, catharsis of all psychical forces.
- Restructuration to completeness (wholeness).
- Building up key qualifications for life and work / business.
- Abilities to master crises, conflicts, disturbances, difficulties and suffering.
- Living rooted in the authentic inner life and balanced with the external life.
- Giving all genuine answers to the mystery of human being and human life.

18. EVOLUTIONARY TURNING POINT

The entire humanity is on an evolutionary path. The

turning point for each human and for the humanity as a whole is characterized by:

- To accept the entire psychical-spiritual life
- To become more and more free from inner burdens of the past life
- To create images in the unconscious to constructively/progressively promote life
- All matters always in communication with the inner Spirit (dreams)
- Regularly gain inner orientation with imagination and contemplation
- Consciously forming all psychical forces and the whole of the psyche (mind)
- Integration of unpleasant matters despite reasoned rejecting facts
- Becoming free from projections and identifications
- Establishing life in the inner life, especially in the power of the inner Spirit

- Living by respecting the values of the psychological-spiritual growing process

- Creating relationship by respecting the psychological-spiritual growing process

- Dealing with the worlds of nature and animals with Spirit and love

- Differentiated development and use of the force of love for everything in life

- Psychical-spiritual performances have highest value and are signed with love

- Resolving conflicts with oneself, with the partner and with the life

- Forming a new human being with inner freedom, with dignity and humility

- Realizing tendencies, talents and potentials through self-education

- High flexibility and inner freedom towards material goods and superficialities

The opposite development of humans is:

→ Unconscious ways of living

→ Driven by desire and prejudgments

→ No inner foundation (roots)

→ Not balanced, not centered

→ Brainwashed, manipulated

→ Build up on lies, disfiguration, distortion

→ No understanding oneself and humans

→ Rooted in illusions, delusion, fabrications

- Philosophical Anthropology is Life Philosophy: oriented on humane qualities, on efficiency, on all-sided balanced mental functions, on meaningful happiness, on holistic satisfaction and fulfillment.

- Philosophical Anthropology is Life Philosophy: Life Philosophy requires human values, knowledge, skills, and a holistic mental development embedded in the manifold environmental and social systems.

- **The Modern Philosophical Anthropology leads to an understanding of humans and human life that is expressed in the Archetypes of the Soul.**

A modern Philosophical Anthropology leads into a conceptual and practical Positive Life Philosophy. A Positive Life Philosophy includes efficient humane attitudes towards human evolution in general and an all-sided personal development in particular:

- Openness to learn & readiness for changes in the personal and collective interest
- Flexible integration of life realities respecting social networks and conditions
- Living with social skills, life techniques, responsibility for health and the environment
- Forming an efficient self-management for life issues, also in matters of human values
- Liberation from the generation-destiny for an evolutionary future

- Establishing a balance between the inner and external life to reduce egoism

- Consciousness about the inner world and the network with external realities

- Understanding humanity as a global organism on a collective spiritual path

- Solidarity with the human community in all genuine human basic needs

- Respecting all human beings in the spiritual view of the collective evolution

- Self-control within the inner and external world for constructive interactions

- Cleaning the subconscious for inner peace and peace in the world

- Dissolution and balance of all contradictory inner forces for peace on earth

- Relevant knowledge about the complexity of inner and external life

- Many-sided consciousness about mankind and the state of the world

- Differentiated perception of one's own reality as well as the reality of others

- Strengthening life energy, using it aim-oriented for a better life and world

- Living consciously with responsibility and love for humanity and the creation

→ Positive Life Philosophy gives direction to life and psychical-spiritual development, founded in the Modern Philosophical Anthropology.

- There is never a sustainable evolution of humans and humanity as a whole without these attitudes and psychical-spiritual performances.

- A human can never find his sustainable happiness and fulfillment of life without such a Positive Life Philosophy because humans are intrinsically 'spiritual' and not simply functional (in psychological and behavioral terms) and biological.

- The alternative to this Positive Life Philosophy is pure sarcasm, psychosis and insanity, the complete perversion of psychical-spiritual evolution, the absolute abuse of humanity for small elites and the authorities of religions, and in the end the destruction of the planet and the elimination of the entire humanity, including the elites.

- Everywhere, in media, politics, economics, public education, academic education (social sciences), spiritual communities, and religions everything about the human's deepest nature, the innermost meaning of life, and the 'evolutionary' way of living is perverted, psychotic, farcical, distorted, fabricated, manipulated, brainwashed, and falsified.

- The truth and the genuine human values on earth have lost, are perverted, and have become outrageously ugly.

> **Life Philosophy is based on:**
>
> The Modern Philosophical Anthropology has herewith proven with its manifoldness of knowledge and interrelatedness, put into a new frame of human evolution, that humanity today has reached a breaking point: the irreversible development towards complete elimination; or a development towards a sustainable human evolution for millenniums to come.

THE FOUNDER

Dr. Edward Schellhammer is the founder and President of the Schellhammer Education Group that includes the Schellhammer Business School, the Schellhammer Institute and the Schellhammer Retreat.

What is most striking about meeting Dr. Edward Schellhammer beyond his pleasant and polite manner; youthful disposition or passionate and sincere views on humanity and the planet, is his unshakable conviction that the world needs a new pioneering education.

But exactly who is Dr. Edward Schellhammer? Is he a Philosopher, an expert on human matters, a Psychologist, a prolific author of over 30 titles from psychology to politics and economics, an educator, or a visionary with a profound and beneficial insight into the human condition?

The answer is that he is all that and more. In different age, he would have been called a polymath, and probably kept close company with those giants of The Age of Enlightenment, like his fellow countryman Jean Jacques Rousseau, Thomas Payne and perhaps even Thomas Jefferson. For, it is exactly this gift of enlightenment that Dr. Schellhammer wants to give humanity.

He reveals: "My studies, global travels, professional experiences and extensive study and research since 1970 have given me a clear and unique insight into humanity, human evolution, spirituality, education, cultures, needs, values, standards and our purpose in life like no other!"

Pausing to add: "Humanity hasn't even begun to discover what the true path of human life on earth is fundamentally good and right for".

Born and educated in Switzerland he has lived in

Paris, South of France, London, Kiel, Detroit, and Mexico, before settling in Marbella, Spain, some 27 years ago.

He studied Education, Psychology, Psychoanalysis, and Philosophy. He was a lecturer at the University of Zurich as well as other institutions, and as a member of international workshops he dedicated his ample energy to futurology, future perspectives of humanity, peace and disarmament, development of education in Latin America and key global issues in general, concentrating on developing a new understanding of politics and economics for the future. His findings are indispensable for all those who value life, love, and justice.

He places great emphasis on Dream Theory a subject that he has researched for most of his life and passionately believes in, declaring that some 35 years ago he had a dream that told him to solve the mystery of man and human evolution. Stating categorically: "My initial reaction was, this is an impossible task!" and then quickly adds with equal conviction: "But today, I think, no, I know, that I have discovered all the fundamental components that explain the mystery of man and human evolution."

With his professional background, he has written many books spanning: Individuation (holistic personal development), Dream Theory and Interpretation, Problem Solving, The Individual and Collective Unconscious, Love and Relationships, The Archetypes of Man, The Future of Humanity, Global Human Education, New Philosophical Anthropology, Didactics in Teaching and Counseling and Coaching.

All inner processes – psychical, spiritual and practical – to find and live the (archetypal) codes of human evolution are well documented like never before in the history of mankind. Everything that you need to learn is elaborated in his books.

Dr. Edward Schellhammer has unveiled the mystery of mankind, the psychological-spiritual and archetypal codes of human evolution. It has taken 35 years to understand humans, the divine and factual human evolution, the mendacious aims of politics, economy, public education, religion, spirituality, and the state of humanity and the world, in order to offer you today the eternally valid concept (codes) of the Archetypal Human Evolution.

During the last 35 years he had around 14,000 dreams about the state and development of humanity, the world and the planet. Countless dreams have shown him everything of fundamental relevance for humanity's future and evolution.

During the same period, he also had estimated 3,000 dreams about the genuine archetypal evolution of mankind, the state and potentials of the mind and of the world population, the 'other world' and God. He has been in his dreams in the 'other world', in the divine paradise, and he has experienced the 'Union with God' as well as many more archetypal processes. He profoundly elaborated all this; estimated 80,000 hours of explorations and analysis in total.

Dr. Edward Schellhammer says: "The never achieved most advanced psychological, spiritual, archetypal, educational and practical concept, the Philosophical Anthropology of the Archetypal Human Evolution, is prepared and can lead humanity to hope, peace, justice, balance, truthfulness, and fulfillment."

Like the man himself his books are not for the faint hearted with challenging, pioneering and vanguard content and new ways of thinking that covers shaping of the mind, personal development, human values, human evolution, life, business, politics, economy, society, education, and religion – for everybody that is searching for the truth and for a fundamental personal fulfillment. Reading his books is pure adventure for the mind.

After decades of extensive explorations, research, analysis, writing and sometimes personal retreat, Dr. Edward Schellhammer is now at the disposal of discerning individuals and institutions wishing to pursue prepared and tailor-made programs of evolutionary further education.

HUMANITY NEEDS A NEW CONCEPT FOR 'MANKIND', A NEW SPIRITUALITY, AND A NEW BREED OF EVOLUTIONARY HUMANS!

HUMANITY NEEDS A NEW GENERATION OF ALL-ROUND PREPARED LEADERS IN EVERY FIELD OF HUMAN ENDEAVOR!

HUMANITY NEEDS A NEW CONCEPT OF BUSINESS SCHOOLS, OF UNIVERSITIES, AND OF A NEW PUBLIC EDUCATION!

HUMANITY NEEDS TO RECLAIM THE ARCHETYPAL SPIRITUALITY ('RELIGION') THAT WAS NEVER ESTABLISHED IN THE PAST!

17.04.2011 I dreamt: "The door to Paradise must now be completely closed for all souls, until the complete enlightenment of the truth is fulfilled globally." Therefore, with all the power of attorney from my spiritual (archetypal) authority [that has given it to me in dreams] and in order to save the human evolution I decide today:

I will not let a single soul into Paradise, apart from a few exceptions, until the deicide octopus is detected and disclosed, until the truth is researched and clarified and put on the table, and until both are fully understood by the entire humanity. Everyone is summoned to work on this catharsis and renewal: Researchers, experts, scientists, journalists, politicians, legal professionals, CEOs, and all varieties of power holders and religious officials; but also, all and every single citizen of all states and nations.

"As the highest judge of all souls living in the other world and of all souls living today and in the future on this earth, I will severely punish the supreme masters of deicide with a minimum of 50,000 years being far away from God and his light, the protagonists with a minimum of 10,000 years, and all other significant collaborators of deicide will not see God and his light for a very long time. People that are unwilling to learn and to develop themselves psychically and spiritually and those who infect the collective (entire societies) with brainwashing, lies and falseness, with their insane narcissism, perverse neurosis, psychosis, psychopathy and madness cannot expect to be allowed to enter into paradise. It is said since millenniums: If a folk and its government ignore its new (genuine, provable) prophet, destroy his life, bans him, and paralyzes with that his divine mission for humanity and the archetypal human evolution, this folk will lose its land. Switzerland is already sentenced. The same punishment is applied for any folk that acts in the same way against this prophet for humanity in the third Millennium. If all of humanity accepts the deicide simply by ignoring it, then most souls will be sent for 200,000 years to a dark place far away from the paradise of God."

THE FOUNDATON FOR A NEW PATH

THE MANIFESTO (ISBN: 1494855917): The book unveils the state of people, of humanity, of the world and the planet. People destroy the evolution of humanity with their blinded religious, atheist or other mental or political insanity. The Manifesto puts the challenge on the table, as never before! Not wanting to know is a shame. How can you be happy with a suppressed shame? You can only become free inside with knowledge, critical thinking, and self-contemplation. This book tells you the 'truth' about the world and the lost archetypal path of humanity!

ARMAGEDDON OR EVOLUTION (ISBN: 1484868668): There are only two options: Humanity's leaders take responsibility to manage evolution in a sustainable manner, or the systemic fissures will crush mankind and the planet will degenerate. The book reveals how everybody can contribute to a sustainable human life. Why should you have a good life if you don't contribute for a better world? The book contains all you need to know about the species called 'human': fulfilling ways of living, evolutionary personality development, man-woman-relationship aiming for 'completeness', a substantial advanced philosophy about humans, and a realistic overview of the big problems around the globe.

THE FUTURE IN YOUR HANDS (ISBN: 1478377917): The truths and facts are outrageous and beyond all imagination. The damages worldwide are monstrous. Everybody pays with their taxes during centuries for ignoring the ongoing massive destruction and wars. Nevertheless, everybody can contribute to create a new path for humanity. The state of humanity and the world - preprogrammed from previous generations - shows us that most parents don't care about what the future will bring to their children. If parents don't care about the future of their children, then the young generation must learn to take their future into their own hands!

DEICIDE (ISBN: 1478366524): Indicted: The supreme masters of neo-capitalism, the leaders of corporations, banks, politics, media, justice, the ultra-high net worth individuals, the leaders of education, universities, Christianity; humans that destroy the genuine human values and that accept the lies as the truth. Those who seriously want to understand the mess also get the conceptual solutions. A must read for all those who work in the education sector, in politics, economy or religion.

BECOME A STRONG PERSONALITY (ISBN: 1478372958): The book provides everything that all people must develop for a sustainable inner foundation in order to be prepared for a fast-changing world. It is ridiculous and stupid if you do not want to become a genuine, strong personality. Read this to prepare yourself for the world!

LOVE YOUR LIFE (ISBN: 1478372834): Everybody needs to build up the ability to love, and to live joy of life. The book provides everything that must be developed in order to find happiness. Most people do not have the slightest idea what love is about. It's much more than an emotion. A must for anyone interested in genuine love!

60 DAYS TO PARADISE (ISBN: 1480177369): Everybody needs to learn about how to develop a better life. The book provides countless tips and practical suggestions to reach genuine success. The paradise is within you. Therefore: Do you want darkness and the hell inside or the eternal sun? You will find out how to create your inner sun.

PRACTICAL PSYCHOLOGY (ISBN: 147836694X): The book provides immense knowledge about humans, human life and human concerns; countless exercises promote personal development, a better life, and professional competences in matters of human life. 90-95% of all humans are archaic humans like people who lived 1000 and 2000 years ago. It is really urgent that you evolve with this book to a very valuable inner status of quality and being.

PSYCHOLOLGY I (ISBN: 1478370661): This book expands the frame of 'Practical Psychology' and presents more precise knowledge about matters of human life and the mind. A lot of practical exercises allow one to reach a high level of genuine personal development. Read rubbish and live with delusions. Remain ignorant. Or take this book in your hands and start becoming a complete and fulfilled human with a precious soul and efficient mind.

POLITICS (ISBN: 1480198714): Politics has failed in

achieving peace on earth, in eliminating the roots of all wars, in creating economic balance, and in promoting human evolution. Outrageous failure! The world needs 10 million and more new politicians and leaders with all-encompassing advanced knowledge and the right personal development. Before you talk about politics and leadership, read this book!

ECONOMICS I (ISBN: 1478226730): The book unveils the dogma and ideology of the biggest scam in modern history that led to the degradation of humanity and the planet via 'profits at all costs'. All business people and those who work in a field of the economy must know what the academic education does not tell you. If you don't want to know, you are a collaborator of the collective destruction.

ECONOMICS II (ISBN: 1478244577): The book delves into the key elements of microeconomics and their intricate relation to financial crises and the omnipresent destructivity exerted on humanity. This book teaches you what you will not learn in accredited economic teaching. Become a robot and servant of the capitalist cynicism or learn about the lies and scams for a new economic world.

ECONOMICS III (ISBN: 1478275626): The book uncovers key facts and figures of the state of humanity and the planet; revealing herewith the systemic failures in economics, politics, education and religion. Not wanting to know about the roots of failures in the economy, in politics, education and religion serves the hidden masters, which systematically destroy the archetypal (genuine) human development. Therefore: Expand your view and serve the human development!

MODERN DREAM THEORY (ISBN: 1478384891): Dreams guide people to the truth, to the power of the inner Spirit. Dream form the ethical, psychological, spiritual and religious foundation of life. Dream shed light on all the principles of the psychical-spiritual growth. Without the 'Spiritual intelligence' of dreams, people can never find fulfillment. There is no better guidance for everyone, regardless of culture, religion or ideology. There is no future for humanity, without taking the power of the inner Spirit seriously.

200 WAYS TO SAVE THE PLANET (ISBN: 1548039209): "Humanity has 25 years left to implement relevant and all-encompassing changes, but must start now." Herein, Dr. Schellhammer outlines 200 concrete ways of practical change for every human being around the globe that can guarantee a change from the cataclysmic roller coaster ride that humanity finds itself on today to a complete renewal in order to bring humanity "back to the path of (archetypal) genuine human evolution," he says.

SCHELLHAMMER RETREAT

The Schellhammer Retreat is an educational institution that offers a one-of-a-kind Retreat together with a unique self-development educational program. The Schellhammer Retreat is about discovery, spirituality, fulfillment and self-exploration through the process of Individuation. Participants are offered a breakthrough in their personal life, fulfillment in their vocation, a deeper archetypal meaning of life, an inner catharsis, and the complete absolution.

The Schellhammer Retreat is a psychical-spiritual 'Life School' that can lead individuals to high and very high aims of the Individuation Process. It includes the shaping processes of any kind of mission for humanity and the genuine (archetypal) human evolution.

Book yourself a stay: SchellhammerRetreat.com.